NOTE TO PARENTS

Welcome to Kingfisher Readers! This program is designed to help young readers build skills, confidence, and a love of reading as they explore their favorite topics.

These tips can help you get more from the experience of reading books together. But remember, the most important thing is to make reading fun!

Tips to Warm Up Before Reading

- Ask your child to share what they already know about the topic.
- Preview the pages, pictures, sub-heads and captions, so your reader will have an idea what is coming.
- Share your questions. What are you both wondering about?

While Reading

- Stop and think at the end of each section. What was that about?
- Let the words make pictures in your minds. Share what you see.
- When you see a new word, talk it over. What does it mean?
- Do you have more questions? Wonder out loud!

After Reading

- Share the parts that were most interesting or surprising.
- Make connections to other books, similar topics, or experiences.
- Discuss what you'd like to know more about. Then find out!

With five distinct levels and a wealth of appealing topics, the Kingfisher Readers series provides children with an exciting way to learn to read about the world around them. Enjoy!

Ellie Costa, M.S. Ed.
Literacy Specialist, Bank Street School for Children, New York

KINGFISHER READERS

level 5

Record Breakers
The Fastest

Brenda Stones

KINGFISHER
NEW YORK

KINGFISHER
LONDON & NEW YORK

Distributed in the U.S. and Canada by Macmillan,
175 Fifth Ave., New York, NY 10010

Library of Congress Cataloging-in-Publication data
has been applied for.

Series editor: Thea Feldman
Literacy consultant: Ellie Costa, Bank St. College, New York

ISBN: 978-0-7534-6907-1 (HB)
ISBN: 978-0-7534-6908-8 (PB)

Kingfisher books are available for special promotions
and premiums. For details contact: Special Markets
Department, Macmillan, 175 Fifth Ave., New York, NY 10010.

For more information, please visit www.kingfisherbooks.com

Printed in China
9 8 7 6 5 4 3 2 1
1TR/0712/UG/WKT/105MA

Picture credits
The Publisher would like to thank the following for permission to reproduce their material. Every care has been taken to trace copyright holders. However, if there have been unintentional omissions or failure to trace copyright holders, we apologize and will, if informed, endeavor to make corrections in any future edition.
(t = top, b = bottom, c = center, r = right, l = left):
Cover Corbis/Larry W. Smith/epa, Corbis/Dean Lewis, Corbis/Bettman, NaturePL/Dave Watts;
Pages 4tl Alamy/Juniors Bildarchiv; 5br Corbis/Bettmann; 7b Alamy/Tom Craig; 8 Corbis/Stephane Cardinale; 9 Corbis/Schlegelmilch; 10b Corbis/Dean Lewis; 11t Alamy/www.gerardbrown.co.uk; 11b Shutterstock (SS)/Jacek Chabraszewski; 12 Corbis/Bettman; 13tl Corbis/Stephen Hird/Reuters; 13c Corbis/Stephen Hird/Reuters; 14cl Corbis/Michael Nicholson; 16 Corbis/UMA/PCN; 17 Getty/Sung-Jin Kang; 18c Corbis/Gopal Chitrakar/Reuters; 18–19 SS/Dimtry Pichungin; 20cr Getty/MLB Photo Archive; 20bl Getty/Lakruwan Wanniarachch/Reuters; 21 Getty/Patrick Kovarik/AFP; 22 Getty/AFP; 23tl Getty/Bloomberg; 23cr Corbis/Larry W. Smith/epa; 24 Corbis/Olivier Maire/epa; 25t SS/Jonathan Larson; 25b Corbis/Xu Jiajun/Xinghua; 26 Frank Lane Picture Agency (FLPA)/Fritz Polking; 29t FLPA/Willi Rolfes/Minden; 29b SS/Sebastian Knight; 31c NaturePL/Brandon Cole; 31b NaturePL/ Wild wonders of Europe/Zankl; 34l, 34c & 34r NaturePL/Dave Watts; 35 Science Photo Library/Harvard College Observatory; 36 SS/SergeyIT; 37 AP/Press Association Images; 38 Corbis/Hannibal Hanschke; 39t Getty/Anwar Hussein; 39b Getty/Dan Kitwood; 40 SS/agophoto; 41 SS/Jeremy Richards; 42c Corbis/Shannon Stapleton/Reuters; 42b Corbis/Enrique de la Osa/Reuters; 43t Corbis/Esa Alexander/Reuters; 43b Corbis/Murad Sezer/Reuters; 44tl SS/Nikonov; 44bl SS/Peter Wollinga; 44br SS/Studio37; 45 Getty/Mario Tama. All other images Kingfisher Artbank.

Contents

The history of speed

People have always wanted to travel faster. First they went faster by riding a camel or a horse. Then they used horses to pull carriages with wheels. People also loaded cargoes onto boats and used the power of the wind to travel across the sea.

People can reach speeds of almost 45 mph (70km/h) on horseback.

Clippers sailed across the seas powered by wind.

Then **steam power** was invented and used to run the first steam trains.

Robert Stephenson's *Rocket* reached 29 mph (47km/h) at its launch in 1829.

Next the motor car was designed, with its **internal combustion engine**. Karl Benz's **automobile** of 1893 reached only 11 mph (17km/h), but after that cars got faster. Finally the airplane was developed, and then space travel.

Karl Benz and his daughter Clara in 1893

World speed records

People keep trying to break the world speed records for traveling on land and water and through the air.

In 1964, British driver Donald Campbell broke both land and water world records. He set the water record at 276 mph (444km/h) in his boat *Bluebird K7*, and the land record at 429 mph (690km/h) in his car *Bluebird CN7*. Campbell was killed while traveling at more than 300 mph (480km/h) on a lake in England.

In 1997, the British driver Richard Noble broke the land speed record and the **sound barrier** by driving at 763 mph (1,228km/h) in his jet-propelled *ThrustSSC*. A jet-propelled car is one that has a **jet engine**.

The British-built *ThrustSSC*.
SSC stands for supersonic car.

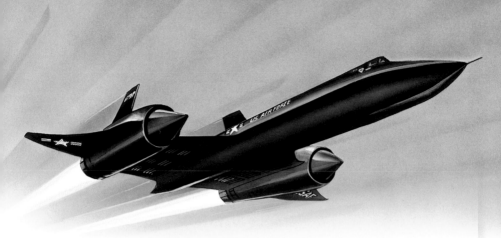

The U.S. Air Force's SR-71 "Blackbird" last flew in 1999. *ThrustSSC* and the SR-71 are very similar in shape.

Ken Warby from Australia set a new world water speed record in 1978, zooming along at 318 mph (511km/h) in a jet-powered **hydroplane**.

The flight speed record is held by American pilot Eldon Joersz, who in 1976 flew the jet-powered SR-71 "Blackbird" at 2,193 mph (3,326km/h)—3.3 times the speed of sound.

On rails
The world train speed record was set in 2007 by the French **TGV**, which sped along at 357 mph (574km/h).

Motor racing

Formula 1, or F1, is the top class of motor racing in the world. The "formula" is a set of rules which all competitors must follow.

The F1 races are called **Grands Prix**. They are usually held on special tracks but are sometimes run on streets that have been closed to the public.

Prizewinners

At the end of the F1 season, there are two prizes—one for the best driver and one for the maker of the winning car.

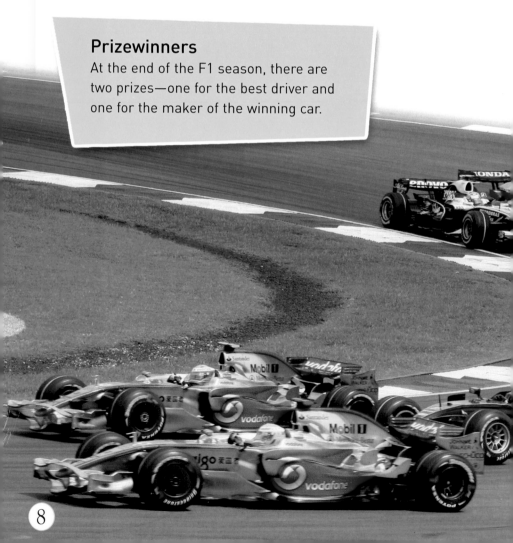

How do you win at Formula 1?
One of the trickiest tactics in the race is overtaking. This is the only way you can get past your competitors.

The cars race at speeds of up to 240 mph (386km/h), powered by engines that turn at 18,000 **rpm**. The cars go faster because of their **aerodynamic** shape, the **suspension**, and the strength of the tires.

Pedal power

People want to travel as fast as they can on bicycles too! The **penny farthing** was one of the earliest bicycles invented in 1871. This was the first bicycle to have tires made of rubber. Its first speed record was just 15.8 mph (25.5km/h).

This bicycle was named after two British coins of different sizes—the penny and the farthing.

Today bicycles go pretty fast. Cyclists ride **carbon fiber** bicycles, and can reach speeds of 32 mph (52km/h). One cycling record is the 500-meter flying start. In this race, the cyclist is already cycling fast when he or she passes the start line. In 2007, British cyclist Chris Hoy set a world record for the 500-meter flying start, at 24.758 seconds.

Matthew Crampton, Chris Hoy, and Jason Kenny racing in 2007's World Cup in Sydney, Australia

A recumbent bike has a more comfortable seat and handlebars than a racing bike does.

In the 1970s, a new design of **recumbent** bicycle appeared. The rider pedals lying down, so there is less **wind resistance**.

How fast are you on a bicycle?
Time yourself riding over a fixed distance and see if you can improve your speed.
What makes you go faster?

Fastest on water

There are all kinds of speed records for boats. The Blue Riband is an award for the fastest passenger ship to cross the Atlantic ocean. This record has been held by the SS *United States* since 1952.

The SS *United States* set the speed record for sailing both eastward and westward.

There have been plenty of records set by sailboats. In 1967, the British sailor Francis Chichester became the first person to sail **solo** around the world, taking 9 months, 1 day.

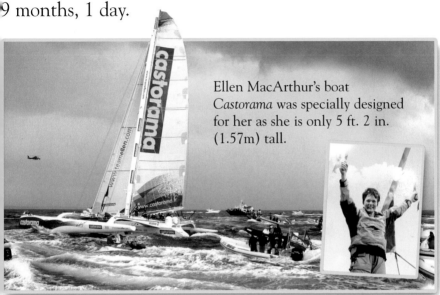

Ellen MacArthur's boat *Castorama* was specially designed for her as she is only 5 ft. 2 in. (1.57m) tall.

Since then, the technology of sailboats has improved immensely. In 2001, Ellen MacArthur, from Great Britain, became the first woman to sail solo around the world. Then, in 2005, she set a world record of 71 days, 14 hours, 18 minutes, 33 seconds. This was broken in 2008 by the French sailor Francis Joyon, who cut 14 days off MacArthur's time.

Did you know?
Sailing around the world westward takes twice as long as sailing around eastward because the tides and winds slow you down.

Fastest in air and space

The Wright brothers made the first successful powered flight in 1903. Their plane only just cleared the ground, traveling at a speed of 6.8 mph (10.9km/h).

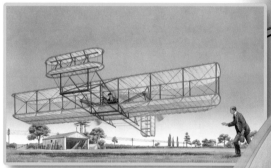

American brothers Wilbur and Orville Wright made their first successful flight in a biplane called the *Flyer* (above).

The first solo flight across the Atlantic was made by the American Charles Lindbergh in 1927 and took 33.5 hours. By 2003, Concorde could cross the Atlantic in 2 hours, 52 minutes, 59 seconds.

Cruising at speed
Concorde's average cruising speed was 1,330 mi. (2,140km) an hour.

Voyager 1 flew past both Saturn
and Jupiter, taking photos.

To leave the **atmosphere** and fly into space, a
spacecraft has to travel much faster than an ordinary
airplane. The fastest manned vehicle in space was
Apollo 10, which reached 24,791 mph (39,897km/h) in
1969.

In 1980, *Voyager 1*, an unmanned spacecraft, flew
at 38,352 mph (61,722km/h).

The fastest human-made object in space was *Helios 2*,
sent to study the Sun in 1976. It flew at 157,078 mph
(252,792km/h) and reached the Sun in three months.

Running and swimming

Running is the fastest way we can move on land without using any form of transportation. When we talk about "the fastest man on Earth" we usually mean the best sprinter over a short distance. Today the fastest man on Earth is the Jamaican Usain Bolt, who set world records of 9.58 seconds over 100 meters and 19.19 seconds over 200 meters in 2009.

Bolt at the 2009 World Athletics Championships in Berlin, Germany

Ian Thorpe set 18 individual world records between 1999 and 2002. He retired from swimming at the age of 24 but in 2011 started training again, ready for the 2012 Olympics.

The Australian Ian Thorpe, "the Thorpedo," holds the record for being the fastest 14-year-old in the history of swimming. In 1998, at age 15, he became the youngest world champion ever when he won the 400-meter **freestyle** in Perth, Australia.

Which is the fastest stroke?

1 front crawl: 7.831 feet (2.387 meters) per second
2 butterfly: 7.142 feet (2.177 meters) per second
3 backstroke: 6.703 feet (2.043 meters) per second
4 breaststroke: 6.033 feet (1.839 meters) per second

Climbing and falling

Some people run up mountains. The American climber Sean Burch ran up Mount Kilimanjaro in Africa in a record 5 hours, 28 minutes, 48 seconds!

The record speed for climbing Mount Everest—the world's highest mountain, is also impressive. In 2004, Nepalese climber Pemba Dorje Sherpa climbed from base camp to the summit in 8 hours, 10 minutes, breaking the record held by Lakpa Gelu Sherpa by 2 hours.

Pemba Dorje Sherpa

Joseph Kittinger
just after he
jumped out of
the balloon

Can you imagine **freefalling** in space? In 1960, the American pilot Joseph Kittinger broke all the records. He jumped out of a balloon and fell for 4 minutes, 36 seconds, reaching a speed of 614 mph (988km/h), before opening his parachute at 18,000 feet (5,500 meters). This was the fastest a human had ever traveled through the atmosphere.

The summit of
Mount Everest,
29,029 feet (8,848
meters) high

Fastest ball games

What is the fastest baseball pitch ever thrown? The record is 100 mph (162.4km/h), set by the American player Nolan Ryan while playing for the California Angels in 1974.

Cricket sees fast balls as well. The fastest ball ever bowled was by Shoaib Akhtar of Pakistan in 2003. The ball traveled at 100.2 mph (161.3km/h).

Akhtar is nicknamed "the Rawalpindi Express" after his hometown.

Tennis players hit the ball with a racket to make it travel faster. The Croatian player Ivo Karlovic holds the world record for the fastest tennis serve. In 2011, he served a ball at 156 mph (251km/h). The women's record for the fastest serve is held by the American player Venus Williams. In 2007, she served a ball at 129 mph (208km/h).

Nolan Ryan throwing a fast baseball pitch, this time for the Texas Rangers

Venus Williams serves

Fastest scoring

In soccer and football, players need to score to win the game! Sometimes they do so very quickly. Here are some records for the soccer World Cup.

Fastest goal after kickoff: Hakan Sükür of Turkey in 11 seconds (2002).

Fastest goal in a final: Johan Neeskens of the Netherlands in 90 seconds (1974).

Fastest soccer hat trick (three goals): László Kiss of Hungary in 8 minutes (1982).

Fastest ejection (sending off): José Batista of Uruguay after 56 seconds (1986).

Neeskens's rapid goal was scored with a penalty kick after less than 2 minutes of play.

Jay Culter (left), the fastest passer in football

Devin Hester (above) made an amazingly fast touchdown in Miami in 2007, but his team still lost the game.

Here are some records for the Super Bowl championship.

Fastest touchdown from start: Devin Hester of the Chicago Bears in 14 seconds.

Fastest field goal: Tony Franklin of the New England Patriots in 1 minute, 19 seconds.

Fastest pass by a quarterback: 63 mph (101km/h) by Jay Cutler, playing for the Denver Broncos, in 2007.

Fastest NFL team to get to the Super Bowl: the Kansas City Chiefs who began in 1960 and played in their first Super Bowl in 1967.

Why do we move fast on skates and skis? The simple answer is that as the skis or skates press down on snow or ice, they make a film of water. This reduces **friction**, so you slide faster.

Speed skiers have helmets to protect their heads and foam pads to protect their legs.

In speed skating, the average speed rose from 28 to 32 mph (45 to 52km/h) from 1971 to 2009. The world speed record for skiing downhill is 156.2 mph (251.4km/h), set by Simone Origone of Italy in 2006.

The Canadian bobsled team race toward a 2006 Olympic silver medal.

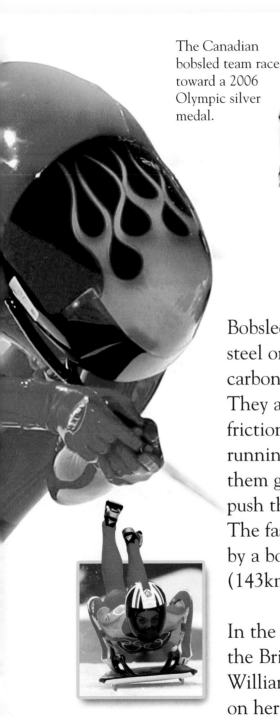

Bobsleds are made of steel on the outside and carbon fiber on the inside. They are designed to reduce friction. Racers wear spiked running shoes to help them grip the track as they push their sled at the start. The fastest recorded speed by a bobsled is 89 mph (143km/h).

Amy Williams winning gold at Vancouver in 2010

In the 2010 Winter Olympics the British racer Amy Williams reached this speed on her **skeleton sled**, winning a gold medal in a record-breaking 53.68 seconds.

Fastest mammals

Which are the five fastest land animals in the world?

Cheetah: 70 mph (113km/h)
Pronghorn antelope: 61 mph (98km/h)
Wildebeest: 50 mph (80km/h)
Lion: 50 mph (80km/h)
Thomson's gazelle: 50 mph (80km/h)

How can a cheetah run so fast? Every part of its body is made for speed. Its body is slender and light, and its long tail helps it stay balanced. Its claws grip the ground and help it push forward, just as a spiked track shoe helps a runner in a race.

From a standing start, a cheetah can **accelerate** to 60 mph (96km/h) in just three seconds. That is faster than most racecars!

The spikes of running shoes work in the same way as a cheetah's claws.

Fastest birds

Which are the five fastest birds?

Peregrine falcon: 117–138mph (188–217km/h)
White-throated needletail: 106 mph (170km/h)
Bewick's swan: 45 mph (72km/h)
Barnacle goose: 42 mph (68km/h)
Eurasian crane: 42 mph (68km/h)

The peregrine falcon flies along at an impressive 117–138 mph (188–217km/h). When it dives, it is faster still. It swoops down on its prey at amazing speeds of up to 242 mph (390km/h).

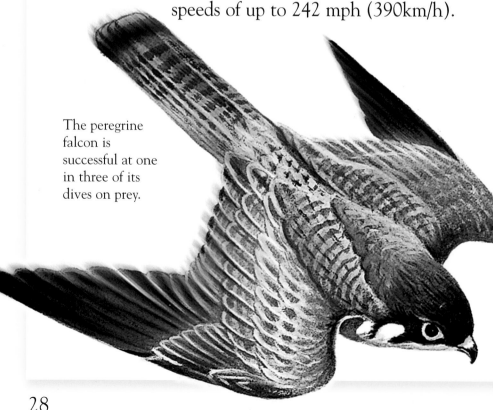

The peregrine falcon is successful at one in three of its dives on prey.

The Eurasian crane can fly across France in less than a day.

Scientists can find out how fast geese fly by fitting them with satellite transmitters.

Flying south for the winter
Barnacle geese live in northern areas in the summer. During the fall, they fly south to spend the winter somewhere warmer.

Fastest fish

Which are the five fastest fish?

Sailfish: 68 mph (110km/h)
Marlin: 50 mph (80km/h)
Wahoo: 48 mph (78km/h)
Southern bluefin tuna: 47 mph (76km/h)
Yellowfin tuna: 46 mph (74km/h)

A sailfish leaps out of the water if it is alarmed, raising its high fin like a sail to frighten its attackers or its prey.

When the sailfish is under the water, its fin is folded down and the sailfish speeds along.

This striped marlin is hunting for sardines in the Pacific Ocean near Mexico.

The marlin swims fastest when it is deep in the water, but it may still be eaten by a shark!

The bluefin tuna travels fast because its body is shaped like a missile.

Fastest dinosaurs

How fast did dinosaurs run?

Compsognathus: approx. 40 mph (65km/h)
Velociraptor: approx. 25 mph (40km/h)
Dilophosaurus: approx. 25 mph (40km/h)
Allosaurus: approx. 22 mph (35km/h)
Tyrannosaurus: approx. 19 mph (30km/h)

How do we know how fast dinosaurs ran? People have found many dinosaur tracks and footprints. Scientists have used these tracks to figure out approximately how fast the dinosaurs moved. These are some of the fastest.

Compsognathus was only the size of a chicken, but it wa a superfast dinosau

Tyrannosaurus

Allosaurus

Dilophosaurus

Velociraptor

Did you know?
All of the fastest dinosaurs were meat eaters.
Their speed helped them catch their prey.

Fastest in nature

There are some record-breaking speeds in nature. They may not change much from year to year, but they are still fast! Here are some fast facts from the natural world.

The fastest hummingbirds can beat their wings 90 times a second, allowing them to hover in one spot in the air while they drink nectar from flowers. This is so fast that we see their beating wings as just a blur.

The fastest insect is the Australian dragonfly, which can fly at 36 mph (58km/h).

The hummingbird's name comes from the humming sound that the bird's wings make while beating so fast.

This Venus flytrap is catching a dragonfly. These plants usually eat small insects such as flies and wasps.

The fastest killer in the plant world is the Venus flytrap, which can close on a mosquito in one-fiftieth of a second!

The fastest-flowing river in the world is the Atrato River in Colombia, South America. Every second, 173,000 cubic feet (4,900 cubic meters) of water flow from the river into the Caribbean Sea.

Star performer
Comets fly at their fastest (300 mi. (482km) per second) when they are near the Sun, and they slow down as they move away. In 1843, one comet broke all records. It whisked around the Sun in 2 hours, 7 minutes at a speed of 589 mi. (948km) per second.

Fastest fingers, fastest brains

We humans can train our brains—and our fingers—to work incredibly fast.

A nine-year-old girl, Nandini Sankhla from India, once memorized a list of 100 objects in 9 minutes, 49 seconds. Afterward, she could remember the list both in the order she learned it and backward.

Txt it!
There are records for fastest texting. The test phrase for texting speed used by the *Guinness Book of World Records* is 160 characters long: *"The razor-toothed piranhas of the genera Serrasalmus and Pygocentrus are the most ferocious freshwater fish in the world. In reality they seldom attack a human."* How fast can you text that? The world record is 34.65 seconds. It was set by Frode Ness in Oslo, Norway, in 2010.

The world record for solving the Rubik's cube is 5.66 seconds. It was set by Feliks Zemdegs of Australia in 2008.

Rubik record

In March 2010, 134 boys from a school in Amersham, England, broke the record for the most people solving a Rubik's cube at once. They did it in 12 minutes.

Fastest sellers

The fastest-selling book ever is a book in the Harry Potter series. In the United States, 8.3 million copies of the final title in the series, *Harry Potter and the Deathly Hallows*, were sold in the 24 hours after it came out.

Eager fans getting their copies of
Harry Potter and the Deathly Hallows

The fastest-selling DVD ever is *Avatar*, which sold 19.7 million copies in three weeks in 2010. This beat *The Dark Knight*, which sold 16 million copies in 2008.

"Candle in the Wind" sold so fast because it was released after Diana, Princess of Wales, died, and people bought it in memory of her.

The fastest-selling music single ever is Elton John's "Candle in the Wind", which sold 3.5 million copies in the United States in its first week in 1997.

The fastest-selling download in the United States is Flo Rida's song "Right Round". In the first week after its release in 2009, 636,000 copies were sold.

Alexandra Burke (right) had the fastest-selling download in Europe after winning the U.K. TV singing competition *The X Factor* in 2008. She also became the first British female soloist to sell one million copies of a single in the U.K.

More and more people!

Can a city be the fastest? Many of the world's cities are growing very fast, as more and more people move to live in them and more and more buildings are built.

Between 2000 and 2010, the number of people living in Guangzhou, China, grew by 3.3 million. The number of people living in Karachi, Pakistan, grew by 3.1 million, and the number of people living in Delhi, India, grew by 2.9 million.

Guangzhou is a busy, fast-growing city.
It has many thriving industries.

The old street market in Delhi teems with people.

Today these three cities are the fastest-growing in the world.

City	3	6	9	12	15
Guangzhou					
Karachi					
Delhi					

Millions of people in 2000	
Millions of people in 2010	

How many people altogether?

At the beginning of 2012 there were about seven billion people in the world. Experts think that this will grow to well over nine billion by 2050.

Crazy speed records

Here are some crazy speed records.

In New York, in 2007, Ashrita Furman broke his own world record for pushing an orange with his nose for a mile. His new record was 22 minutes, 41 seconds.

Ashrita Furman has set 356 official world records since 1979. Here he is pushing an unripe orange with his nose.

Erick Hernandez from Cuba broke the world record for soccerball control in October 2009. He touched the ball 341 times with his head in 60 seconds.

"Flying Phil" Rabinowitz, who stayed fit by walking 4 mi. (6km) every day

South African Philip Rabinowitz set a record as the fastest 100-year-old to run 100 meters, in Cape Town, South Africa, in July 2004. His first bid had failed when a power outage stopped the electronic clocks.

Metin Senturk is a blind Turkish singer who set a world record for driving a car when blind and unaccompanied in April 2010. He reached a speed of 181.99 mph (292.89km/h) in a Ferrari F430 car.

Senturk was guided by a person in a vehicle behind him giving instructions through an earpiece.

43

Or why not slow down?

Let's take a break and celebrate some of the slowest things on Earth.

A crocodile can slow down its heart so that it beats just twice a minute. This lets the crocodile hold its breath for as long as an hour when it is underwater.

A sloth moves so slowly that algae grows on its furry coat.

A seahorse rarely travels faster than 0.01 mph (0.016km/h).

A British fundraiser, Lloyd Scott, set a world record for the slowest marathon, in Edinburgh, Scotland, in 2003. He wore a deep-sea diving suit, like this one, and took 6 days, 4 hours, 30 minutes, 56 seconds to cover the distance.

Snail mail

Ethel Martin of Oberlin, Kansas, received the slowest Christmas card ever. It took 93 years to reach her. Her cousins in Nebraska mailed the card on December 23, 1914 and it finally arrived in December 2007!

Glossary

accelerate to go faster

aerodynamic an aerodynamic shape lets air flow easily past an object so that it can move faster through the air

atmosphere the layer of gases immediately above Earth's surface

automobile another name for a car

carbon fiber a material that is very light in weight and very strong, so it is good for making boats, bicycles, and bobsleds

clippers fast sailing ships in the 1800s that could "clip" or cut through the waves

freefalling falling through the sky without a parachute

freestyle in swimming, freestyle means any stroke. Swimmers usually choose the front crawl for a freestyle race because it is the fastest stroke

friction the force that slows things down and stops their movement

Grand Prix (plural: Grands Prix) the French term for big prize. A Formula 1 motor race is known as a Grand Prix

hydroplane a motorboat that races just above the surface of the water

internal combustion engine an engine that is driven by burning gasoline or diesel with air

jet engine a very fast internal combustion engine that works by ejecting a stream of liquid

penny farthing a bicycle invented in 1871. It was nicknamed the penny farthing because of the size of its wheels; in Great Britain, a penny was a large coin and a farthing was a small coin. The large front wheel helped it go faster and ride over rough surfaces

recumbent being in a lying down position. A recumbent bicycle is one where the rider is in a lying down position

rpm revolutions per minute; the number of times an engine turns over (or revolves)

skeleton sled a small, light sled with no brakes that a person rides face downward

solo one person on their own

sound barrier the point at which a vehicle goes faster than the sound it makes and so becomes supersonic

steam power force or energy produced by heating water

suspension the springs and shock absorbers in a car or bicycle

TGV the French *train à grande vitesse*, which means high speed train

wind resistance the force, or drag, of the wind slowing down a moving object. If a vehicle has an aerodynamic shape, it has less wind resistance

Index

If you have enjoyed reading this book, look out for more in the Kingfisher Readers series!

KINGFISHER READERS: LEVEL 1

Baby Animals
Busy as a Bee
Butterflies
Colorful Coral Reefs
Jobs People Do
Seasons
Snakes Alive!
Trains

KINGFISHER READERS: LEVEL 2

What Animals Eat
Where Animals Live
Where We Live
Your Body

KINGFISHER READERS: LEVEL 3

Ancient Rome
Dinosaur World
Record Breakers—The Biggest
Volcanoes

KINGFISHER READERS: LEVEL 4

Flight
Pirates
Sharks
Weather

KINGFISHER READERS: LEVEL 5

Ancient Egyptians
Rainforests
Record Breakers—The Fastest
Space

For guidance for teachers and parents and activities and fun stuff for kids, go to the Kingfisher Readers website:
www.kingfisherreaders.com